Blowpop

Blowpop

A #Blessed Study Companion

Based on the book
#Blessed Be the Hellbound,
published under the psuedonyms
Uppity Atom and Uncanny Currency
by David J. Shepard

Published by Internet Ouroboros/Ouroboros Press

Original © 2023 Internet Ouroboros/Ouroboros Press / David J. Shepard

This edition © 2024-25
Hardcover ISBN-13: 979-8-9894251-4-3

All content in this publication (design, graphics, text, sounds, pictures, videos, software and other files and the selection and arrangement thereof) are the property of David J. Shepard, dba as Objektv.info®, and are subject to and protected by United States and international copyright and other intellectual property laws and rights.

Some content, whose ownership is retained by its copyright owners, is used based on accepted guidelines for Fair Use (accessed on April 10, 2022 from https://www.copyright.gov/fairuse/more-info.html):

"Section 107 of the Copyright Act provides the statutory framework for determining whether something is a fair use and identifies certain types of uses—such as criticism, comment, news reporting, teaching, scholarship, and research—as examples of activities that may qualify as fair use."

Stock graphics and images have been licensed according to rules governing their use by the publishers.

Enjoy the book without assuming any ownership interest in the content. Permission to reproduce any content requires the permission of David (david@internetouroboros.com). You may not copy, reproduce, distribute, republish, download, perform, display, post, transmit, exploit, create derivative works or otherwise use the content of the site in any form or by any means, without the prior written authorization. Registered servicemarks and trademarks belonging to David J.Shepard include Objektv.info® and SumWorld®. This book is a work of fiction. With the implications of everything that that entails.

First Printing, 2023 ISBN-13: 979-8-9894251-6-7

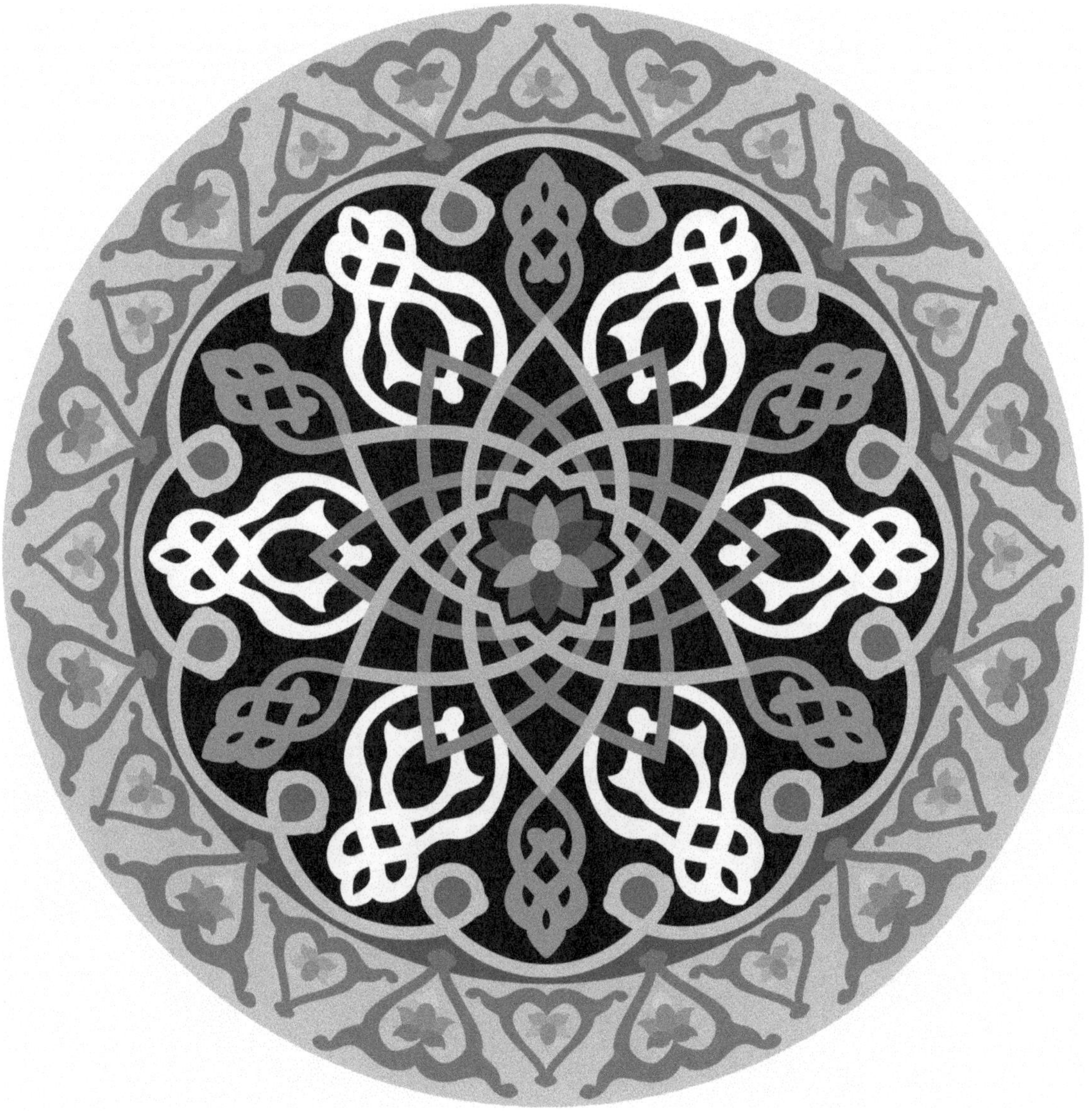

Pre-work

Pre-enact

Existence contains all processes, including death. We, here on earth and in space, are contained by space. Reproductive processes, like other processes, allow for the creative expansion of space to allow us to include others in that space.

These processes include memory, for humans, who now sometimes try to inject their memory into the world and the resulting sensory-rich theater for personal mythology, using the mechanism of a broadcast of limited simultaneity (data storage giving rise to protective acts of constant amputation, in order to meet the demands of commerce). The events that gave rise to us are preceded by impermanence, from where we can observe the events that resolve, for us, in our deaths. Language enables a process of creative expansion of our senses, especially memory, and shared meaning through the creation and circulation of agreement about the meaning of words. Our sense of our distance from those words can transform the meaning those words possess, and the accuity of our senses determines how

much light can be found in the spaces between the characters. ae
If there is a memory of the words that preceded us, grace resides in the memory of the time it took for the word to arrive to us as a shared meaning, and not merely as dead space. Much as the light of the sun does not change its wavelength, only the speed at which it arrives, and then departs.

The longest wavelength? That must be the time it would take becoming us, as a harmonic element of our environment, and the other estimations of the processes involved in being us, beings who as wavelengths have a shared destiny to be consumed in the process of the sun's surrender of heat. Until we can no longer sense energy, or where resides the smallest process our minds can sense (chemical fusion).

Fusion being the aggregation of energy, and þssion being its dissolution through use, improper or otherwise.

Peekaboo! The persistence of connection resides in the proof of a multiplicity of shared connections that communicates awareness: our shared experience of each other and the world.

Be honest: Has the past five years seen a contraction of your sense of the grandeur and sublimity to be found among connections, and theworld in general? A diffusion of the diversity of life? Are you at a crossroads, incapable of forward movement as you are pulled in the three possible directions involving movement that, on earth, can be said to intersect only once? Cerberus awaits on the distant shore?

Scenarios

Cheat sheet! Just a sampling:

• Surrogacy, with Fantasy Induction + Reveal
• Witch Camp, with Fisher Price 'My First Spell' (developed by Big Pharma)
• Ackright, with Performance Management Team (Opportunities to advance)
• KangarooNationwithInductiontoBehavioralModification(Fantasy Objectification and Fetishism with additional supplement. Not legally binding.)
• Luvbaby Liberation Fantasy Reveal, with or without Similac
• Persistence of Stoopid, Ruiner Edition
• Drug-fueled Food Insecurity Crime Spree, with or without Recovery Meds
• Cleanliness/Godliness Connection
• Mike Piazza's Feelings about Belle & Sebastian
• ShowMetheMoney! (SouthofBorderorNorthernLieseditions)
• Phone Tag, Phone Tag Family and Look Who's Coming to Dinner! (Three-part miniseries)
• Test of Regional Knowledge with Local Yocal Coffee Date (Two Player mode)
• Enthusiasms

Complete all challenges for Relationship Pattern Awareness bonus!

How A Family Deals with Rule-based Emotional Responses

or, *How One Family Deals with Autism*

"H" is someone who really believes in and loves following rules. One of his rules is "Tuesday is spaghetti day." He got upset one day when we ran out of noodles, so I made these rules:

~#~

1. Hi, H! Today we are going to list all the rules you live by, one by one. Until we get to the end. It might take a few hours... We'll stop if you get tired!

2. Our list of rules fell into 7 (seven) categories:
• Food
• Playtime
• School
• Friends
• Self-care
• Clothes
• Transportation
• Family

3. Our meeting schedule (H was eager to get to our meeting each day) followed this pattern:

• Months 1-2: "I'll follow rules with you!" And I did!

• Months 2-6: To keep following rules with you, I'll need your permission to break 1 (one) rule a day. You'll get a chance to give permission each time.

• Months 6-48: We got through all of H's rules. I gave him 1 or 2 a month that I asked him to follow with me.

• Months 48-54: H let me know if our new rules worked for him. I asked him if he wanted to make more, and we started talking about why we chose the rules we chose. The first rule: Trust comes first!

~#~

This is just one example of how H and our family decided to address the topic of rules. Obviously, we had the support of trained professionals – medical doctors, our counselor and leaders from our church and community. We always had at least 2 (two) objective adults provide input, e.g., not a parent or community member. Triangulation and isolation feel more dangerous to H than a world without rules.

Communication Impact Theory

This guide outlines how to use "ℏ" (pronounced "hñits") as a form of poly-linguistic measurement that obeys the following rules:
Units of hñits are pluralized using the addition of a vowel or consonant to the front or back of the measure, depending on status of primacy (e.g., unit 1,3,5,7,13 etc.) or odd/evenness, or, in the instance of negative and non-whole numbers, through two-unit prefixes and suffixes. E.g.:

$$£\text{-}ℏ\text{-}æ \text{ or } ø\text{-}ℏ\text{-}üñ, \text{ and } æ 大 \text{-}ℏ\text{-}øя \text{ or } カΣ\text{-}ℏ\text{-}ü 土$$

Units of hñits measure:
Originality of Content: Does this content evoke a sense of novelty in the reader/listener/audience? Multiply for the introduction of joy into the communication.
Ease of Comprehension: Would a typical audience for this communication understand it? Yes!
Polylinguistic Truthfulness: Most importantly, is the logic in the communication apparent to everyone who would or would not use the communication for its intended purpose, i.e., to take a desired or proposed action?

Examples of usage include:
(10ø-ℏ) "We might share a Bauhaus sensibility but we are all gestalt."
(1.4£-ℏ- 大) "You all make me sick to my stomach, not literally but fucking literally!"

CIT - Q&A

Q: Do you ever think of your writing as a painting, which is sleeping gently, which evokes in this all a sense of tenderness like the round shape of eyes on baby mammals?
A: "Ask your mother when she gets home."

Q: How is originality of content relevant to the idea of our collective struggle to depart from our origins?
A: Apparently Billie Holiday was one of the first artists to record covers in a distinctive personal style.

Q: For ease of comprehension, I find the over determination is much more important than cultural or other types of appropriateness in the age of completist postmodernism, so I rate things on a scale of zero to six (0-6), zero to 12 (0-12), puberty and up (P+), adult (A), and tolerant adult (A+).
A: Next question. Good job!

Q: What are the self-reporting hazards of originality in either quantitative or qualitative form? Anecdotal answers are welcome.
A: Either "Language is self-awareness" or "$R_b = \| f(a)/H$".

Explanation, Explained

If we have a basic set of facts, which can be contested or confirmed, what does our decision-making process look like? How do we asses credibility?

Some available options: Scientific Method
Mathematical Proof
Rhetorical Proof

In the scientific method, you use your unbiased observations (unedited) to make hypotheses and then test them against evidence to determine if your results are repeatable.

In geometric (mathematical) proof you explain why you get the results you get by working backwards and explaining the process and logic you used to arrive at your results, including the facts your explanation relies upon.

Reverse engineer your way to a theory by working backwards from a desired interpretation. This method is not scientific (but it's also not uncommon).

Whichever method you use, consideration should be made for:
- Simplicity of explanation
- Degree of intentionality (when describing phenomena that involve agency)
- Repeatability of results
- Understanding of the principles of Causation and Correlation

Section 2

Study Guides

Mental Habits of Lovebaby Liberation

Get thee to a nunnery (sic)

+20 percent MORE curious inquiries!

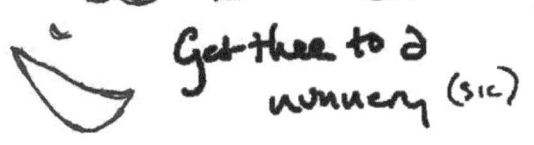

PDA / TLA

COMBINE and INTERLOCK!

If...
This requires a high degree of predictive ability. "Really?"

If... Then
"Predictive ability, predictive schmability, I can see the future!"

* EQ and psychological insight: req'd.

* BOTTLE, DJINN NOT INCLUDED

If only, ... Then
I am reliant on the djinn to make my life happen.

Because you...
✓ You are in control. It will take you x many [xx] additional sentences to incur a penalty stroke

Here's what I see:
We share insights when we want the other person(s) to know we can see who they are in a context defined by the pronoun, "us".

© Vacancy Currency

TRUTH OR CONSEQUENCES ... Sudden Death Edition!

© cc fTW7z
"correct or confirm"

Feeling stuck? The truth will set you free! Or else they'll pay the consequences...

HE WHO BREAKS THE LAW

Laws: Agreed-upon rules that govern our society. When people try to regulate behavior using something other than laws...

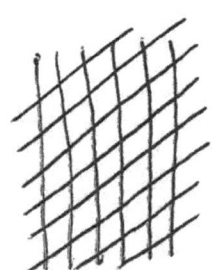

△ There is usually someone willing to accept more restrictive laws for comfort $. This might extend all the way to our most basic rights... Like those protected by the U.S. Constitution.

"This works 4 me b/c I know how it works"

△ I exit through the egress because...
  ○ The longest INT'L flight lasts more than 14 hours. My arms would get tired way before that!
    • Great deal? Some other great deals:
      - Louisiana Purchase
      - Buy One Get One Free!
      - Conversation IRL - no data charges!
      - King, Queen, Jack, Ten, Nine of the same suit
      - Retail therapy in moderation

The scientific method doesn't discriminate. NE1 can use it!

Fictions that Don't/Do Cost Us Rights...

− We don't need to eat food
+ A calorie is a unit of energy needed to turn a certain quantity of food in a pot of boiling water to ash
− You can *never* trust a stranger
+ Any claim to an absolute rule can't be trusted unless proven
+ Wednesday is lasagna day
− Read a Book = You are a Book

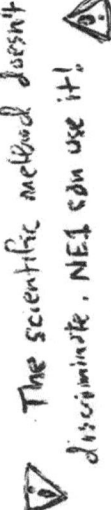

Declaration of Independence RING RING RING

GOAL:

I WANT/MANDATE AN UNCOMPLICATED RELATIONSHIP TO **YOUR** IDENTITY!

- ☐ FETISHIZE
- ☐ OBJECTIFY
- ☐ _____ (OTHER)

Q: IS MY ANXIETY OR FEAR BEING ALIGNED W/ MY WORK, FAMILY OR PLAY? IS YOUR IDENTITY A SOURCE OF ANXIETY IN >1 OF THOSE?

WORK Q: DOES YOUR ID COME W/ A PRESCRIPTION FOR ACTION? WE "SEE" THOSE... IN BEHAVIOR!

PLAY Q: DO I HAVE TO PRETEND I'M 'HAVE A GOOD TIME?'

LOVE Q: IS THIS SCREEN HI-RESOLUTION ENOUGH FOR ME TO SEE ANYONE I DON'T ALREADY KNOW??

✓ TASK LIST:
- ☐ BURY FEELING
- ☐ RESIST SUGGESTION IT EXISTS
- ☐ REPEAT DAILY!

TITLE: IDENTITY BUYER'S REMORSE (LEFT COAST EDITION)

© Uncanny Currency

❝ NEGATIVE INTERNAL NARRATIVE/SELF TALK?? REFLECT 2X A DAY! ❞

🔍 DOES THIS BOX NEED SHADING? OR VIRTUE SIGNALING??

ASSESSM'T (OF STATEMENT) * W/ "ALTRUISM EFFECTS"

- TRUE
  - DENIAL → "LIAR" LABEL, END OF INTIMACY AND/OR TRUST
  - COUNTER
- FALSE (ASSERTION HYPOTHESIS)
  - DENIAL → DEFENSE (IF REASSERT)
  - CORRECTION → WHAT WAS MY ASSUMPTION? → BACK TO ASSESSM'T BY OTHER
    - I AM CORRECT
    - I AM ASSESSING → TRUE ASSESSM'T PATH

EVALUATE FOR:
- NUANCE
- ETC (IRRELEV.)
- BIAS

TEST ASSUMPTION → LOGIC/REASON/PROOF (SCIEN. METHOD) → REVISED ASSESSM'T PATH (RHETORIC)

IRRATIONAL THOUGHT (≠ BE PROVEN EXCEPT THROUGH AMPLIFICATION OR EXTENSION) OR RHETORIC

EARNESTNESS (AS BEHAVIOR OR SPEECH)

EVERYTHING IS BEHAVIOR

ACTING IS "SCRIPTED" → LITTLE SPONTANEOUS ACTION → PERFORMANCE IS "SCRIPTED AND STAGED"

TONE, ACCENT, PERSONA/PERSONALITY and other non-literal language effects (including labeling)

Q: CAN YOU DO THIS REPRESENTING ANOTHER?

THIS IS LEVEL VS. LAYER LOGIC

THE Secret of POGMAHON !!!
(what's your angle?)

(I hear the ocean!)

w/ Dogme 95 Hindsight!

My family said to me:

"You not-round level people need to shove it. If you really claim elevation, try doing your calculations from my Mezzanine, where everything is 1.4888$\overline{333}$," or "one point four eight eight three three three repeating", because you'll be doing those calculations forever in a place I don't want to be with you."

I tried to explain it was a request for dignity which prompted it, not an invitation to hurt. "Everything I love is dear, everything I hate I hurt." Congratulations? I wondered. "Poguemahone."

Priorities - What's important?
Objectives - What do you want to accomplish?
Groupthink, Insight or Future Vision - Past, Present or Future?
Meaning - What does this mean & why?
Analysis - Really? Why do I think so? (Assessment)
Honesty - I'm being honest, about facts and who I represent
Open to change - Are there opportunities to change?
Next steps...

BARRED CODE

© UcJuny Furrency

The Boston we all know and love says "Kiss my ass!" whenever some prick tries to tell you:

Apple = Bandaid because

"There's $$ in that Bandaidstand!"

Home Whites and Away Grays

> TO: Mental Security, MFTP
>
> Waddle into the ocean and evolve, as allowed for by cultural differences in food consumption.

Q: How many ways can you be aware of three (3) things if one (1) of the things you're aware of is your role as observer, while retaining the ability to identify with more than one (1) of them?

A: *(from the chorus)* Simultaneity!

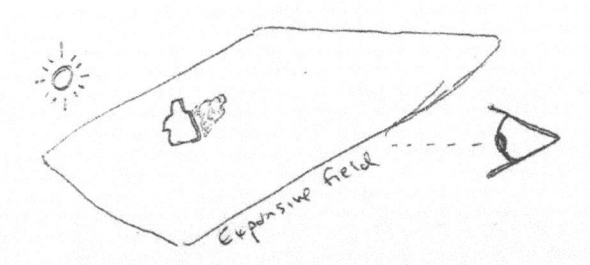

> "That's funny, SNILF*!"
>
> "So?"
>
> *Acronym used with permission from 'Official List of Banned Words'

Get to something "bigger than yourself."

Symbolism: A Funny Definition

"... a more complicated image for a less complicated collection of words"?

E.g., 'Some people thought the numbers 5 and 6 were underused!'

- How many lines in the character?
- Is it a homonym?
- Does it encourage:
  - Spatial relations
  - Emotion
  - Music
  - Basic actions <u>or</u> 'More lines'
  - French kissing 😊

THE PROOF:

Words = An abstraction

Phenomena = Something became real, we describe these as facts

Real = Persistent phenomena, 'Facts made into … [your list of favorite states of matter]'

===

Even in simultaneity, 'You' still persists, doesn't it, good people of 'cogit ergo sum'?

===

Your 'cogit' is a memory of your thoughts. Why don't you try to combine and interlock with that input?

===

'GO FUCK YOURSELF!' was the response.

(LOL, that's a funny proof!!)

The Яussian Dolls...

...visit a venue for the first time*

DOOR – A barrier through which we take a walk to the shore and the sea...

* They choose not to be offended in order to be invited, and enjoy themselves enough to stay! Let us all benefit...

CONTAINER/BASIN – Basins make good reservoirs!

"Let's disobey local snuggling ordinances!"

PILLOW – A seedbed for dreams

SINK – Where the hopes of the *cogit ergo sum* crew meet our shared history...

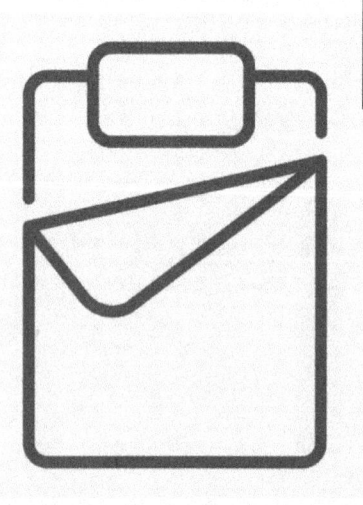

BED – Capable of creating détente and neutralizing gravity or force: an ideal source of the feeling of warmth!

The Delusionator Solution

You Are Here!

REALITY: A physical place where your behavior can be observed by other people.

We do not construct our reality using rules we make or others make for us – we verify reality using the scientific method.

No amount of affection or kindness can make others accept your 'rules for living' if you insist on having them for long enough. We <u>do</u> create rules for society, and we follow them because we see their value: these are called laws. ☺

Delusionator Film Fest

① **Looper** "Persistence matters."

② **Heathers** "Mean Girls suck!"

③ **Shallow Hal** "What measure of a (wo)man?"

④ **Viridiana** "One of us!"

⑤ **Firefly** "Sticks the landing!"

Sponsored by:

- Imaginary Borders Films
- Llorona of the Rules Violations

We Stay Connected Because of...

+ Safety
+ Pleasure of each other's company
+ Emotional connection, especially human touch
+ Collaboration
+ Protection: ourselves or our habitat

Many people stay connected due to a shared interest in prescription eyewear!

What Would You Do If...

... Someone told you that they could become invisible by standing extremely still? And that they do things when they were invisible that you couldn't?

> "I'd ask them how they keep from cramping up!" – *Half Dome, 2011 Rock-climbing Face of the Year*

> "I'd ask if it was actually their perception that changed, and if they stayed invisible even when they moved." – *Samantha Piccolli, Grade 7*

Some think power is derived from size or strength alone – ability (the skills we develop through training and hard work) matters more when we are determined and resilient.

Q: The classroom from Firefly that chooses to lie down is:

a) The First Class
b) The Last Class
c) Precocious Archivists in MPA program
d) Late for Study Hall

FUN FACT: The states that produce the most serial killers per capita are:

1. Alaska – 7.04 per 100k
2. Louisiana – 6.48 per 100k
3. Kansas – 5.24 per 100k
4. Missouri – 5.04 per 100k

Concentric Circles and Meaning

"Meaning is radiating out from our actions!" - every comic book character, ever

Legend of the Cyclops

Mythical creatures the Cyclops tried to prevent the Greek soldier Odysseus's return to his home and family. What was their reason for becoming obstacles? If you knew, you might also be able to defeat them!

Weaknesses:

- Can't Read: The interaction between a book and the reader is complicated. To get better at this skill, you need to learn how to see the world using more than one perspective.

- Kidney Stones: Stones are painful and potentially lethal when thrown! Sticks and stones both can break your bones. But words will never hurt you.

<!> Signs are not present relics of your past desires projected forward <!>

When we think about who we are, we often are forced to use the lenses that language gives us. In English, there are some standard ways to identify people:

- I/Me – 1st Person
- You – 2nd Person
- They/Them – 3rd Person Plural
- Us/We – 1st Person Plural (including the 'Royal We')
- He/Him – Male 3rd Person
- She/Her – Female 3rd Person

If that doesn't make sense, remind yourself from time to time,

"No one else's sensemaking has to make sense to you!"

Intuition can be both a blessing <u>and</u> a curse!

Bless Yourself First!

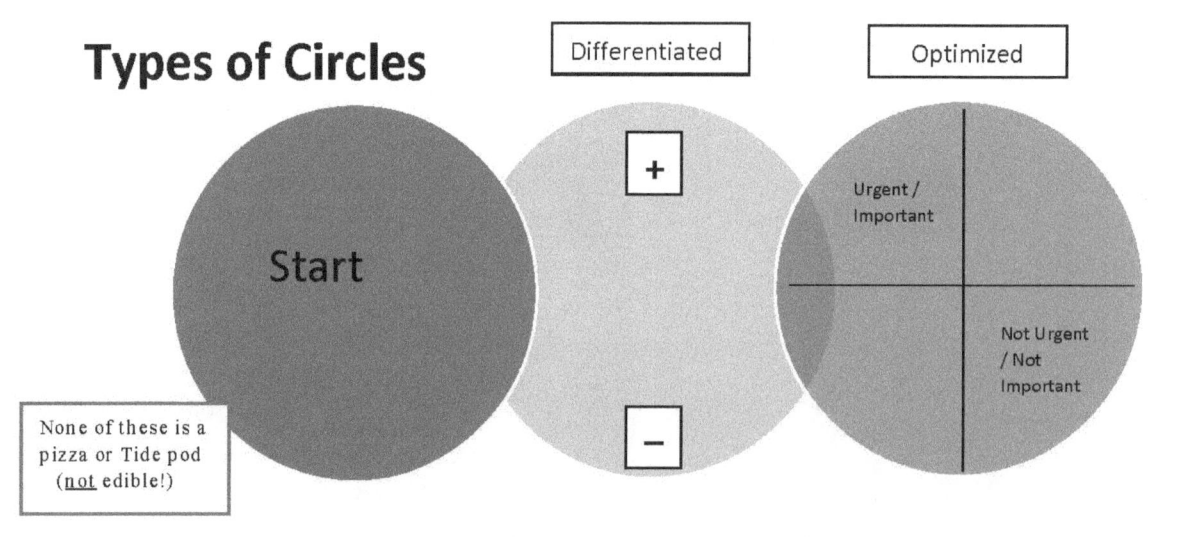

Types of Circles

Differentiated

Optimized

Start

+

−

Urgent / Important

Not Urgent / Not Important

None of these is a pizza or Tide pod (<u>not</u> edible!)

←―――――― Venn Diagram ――――――→

The Death of Intimacy...

- (The Act & Process: Why 'They Suxxx' or Not)

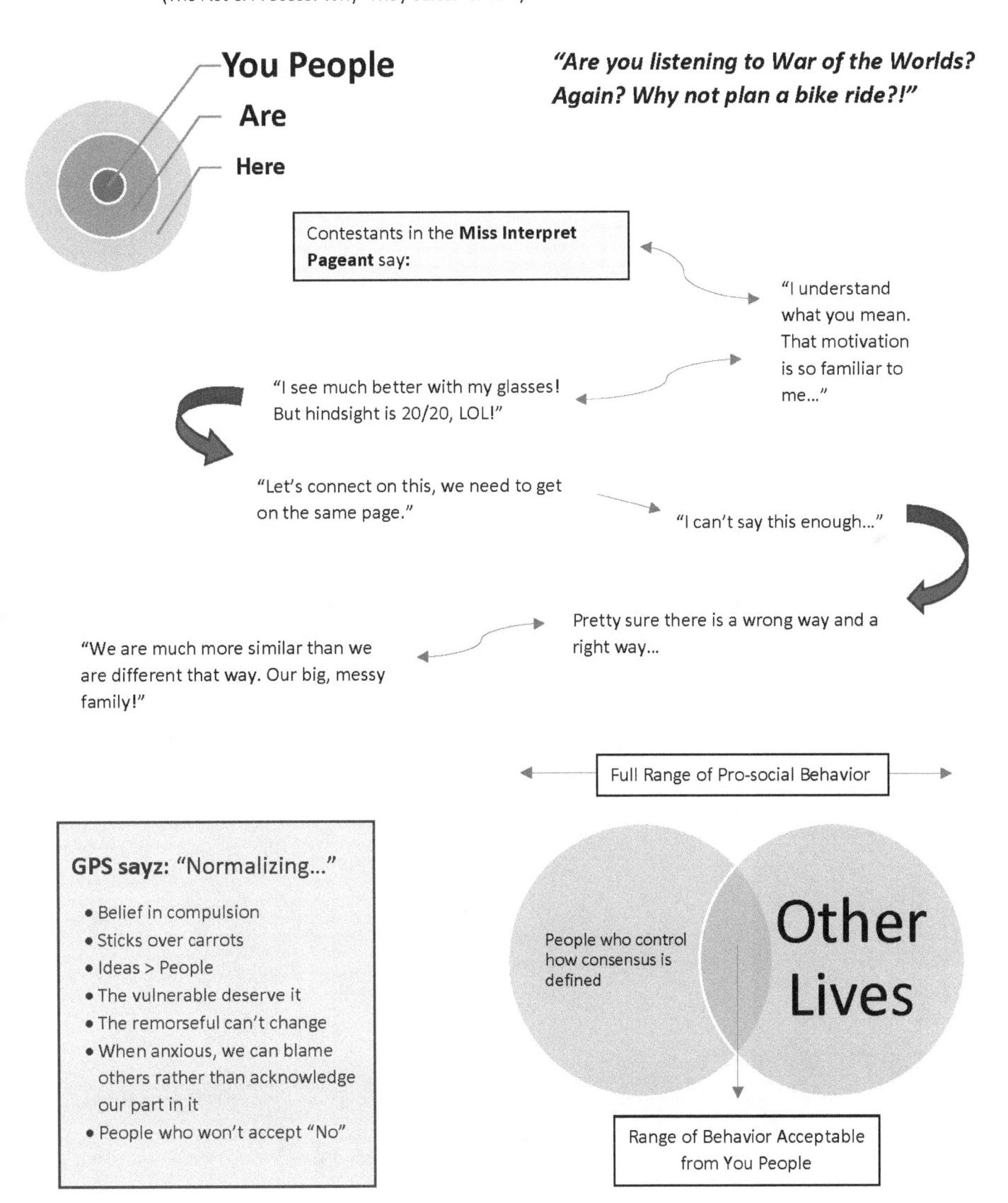

You People
Are
Here

"Are you listening to War of the Worlds? Again? Why not plan a bike ride?!"

Contestants in the **Miss Interpret Pageant** say:

"I understand what you mean. That motivation is so familiar to me..."

"I see much better with my glasses! But hindsight is 20/20, LOL!"

"Let's connect on this, we need to get on the same page."

"I can't say this enough..."

Pretty sure there is a wrong way and a right way...

"We are much more similar than we are different that way. Our big, messy family!"

Full Range of Pro-social Behavior

GPS sayz: "Normalizing..."

- Belief in compulsion
- Sticks over carrots
- Ideas > People
- The vulnerable deserve it
- The remorseful can't change
- When anxious, we can blame others rather than acknowledge our part in it
- People who won't accept "No"

People who control how consensus is defined

Other Lives

Range of Behavior Acceptable from You People

"Just like a unicorn! Just with fewer farts and more magic!"

— William Bard

INNING ONE, PITCHES 1-3

① YOUR MAMA:
"Your mom is so [adjective] that even the finest Islay Scotch whiskeys cannot quench her thirst!" (for example)

② HEIRLOOM TOMATOES:
"Bespoke farm products grace our table while yours is populated by [unsavory food items 1-3]."

③ UNINTENDED CONSEQUENCES:
"When they made you they put mold in the mold!"

INNING ONE, PITCHES 4-6

④ PUNNY STUFF:
"This wall sucks! You have to get under to get over!"

⑤ PULLING RANK:
"You will understand later, if I allow you to get older."

⑥ PULL RANK, AGAIN:
[Sound of your friend slapping themselves in the face]
"Hear me now, believe later."

© 2020 ccFTW72

WHAT IS A CHANGEUP?

A changeup is a way to throw the opposition off balance. Especially when the only language and communication they will accept is:
① What they want;
② Unequal levels of transparency;
③ Something other than <u>clear</u> and <u>direct</u> communication, with attention to the idea there is a person on the other side of the conversation.

CHANGEUPS CAN BE:
① Scripted/planned (blech!);
② Ironic;
③ Playful, especially when they involve plays on meaning.

A BRIEF HISTORY OF THE 3-PITCH IMMACULATE INNING

INNING ONE, PITCHES 7-9

⑦ BAIT AND SWITCH:
[Person divides cookie in unequal halves]
"Whoever divided the cookie chooses halves last!"

⑧ GAMEIFICATION:
"Submit w/ honor to a duel! I declare a thumb war..."

⑨ TRUTH OR CONSEQUENCES, TRUTH OR DARE:
"You get your self-respect back when you submit with honor..."

In Support of Our BASICbot Future

- A Meek Mill/Belinda's Great Foundation and Pre-industrial Lite Magic Co-production

"A solution for our demographic fears!"
— Uppity Atom

"Awww, it's a little half-dead Blackie drone..."
— Count Chocodrac

If you've ever uttered the words 'I don't like it,' then this unit of the #blowpop curriculum is for you! Help us help you validate your "Life in my bubble" beliefs until you use all your data...

The Equation:

$$F - WC/PNW - WZ - H - POC - \sqrt{-1}$$

Use order of operations to disentangle this tricky equation!

- "i" is not a real number
- POC locates someone in an aesthetic, not a community in any historical way
- True or False: Spirituality is our impulse to conform and obey
- Layer of 'Reductive Zen' makes spirituality seem like a predetermined product of age and investigation
- The WC/PNW weather hazards range from light rain to forest fires: LOGIC CONFLICTS emerge from studies in contrast
- LOGIC CONFLICT: Let's use the source of our issues (process) to mask the results of our process (lack of progress)
- $\sqrt{-1} = \textit{"We will return!"}$

'Race As a Predictive Mechanism' Causes a LOT of Conflict:

Logic Conflicts (around expectation and behavior) that ignore the ways institutions and organizations use ethnic/racial identity to curtail non-stereotypical self-expression creates cover for faked or false identities.

A false identity feels false because it consists of things bought, borrowed or stolen – as opposed to lived – and these false identities support false depictions of the state of justice, fairness and equity.

⚠️ Abuse of power to pursue personal goals in the name of social justice ("justice for me") are only available at extra cost, or as a loyalty promo (see directions for offer).

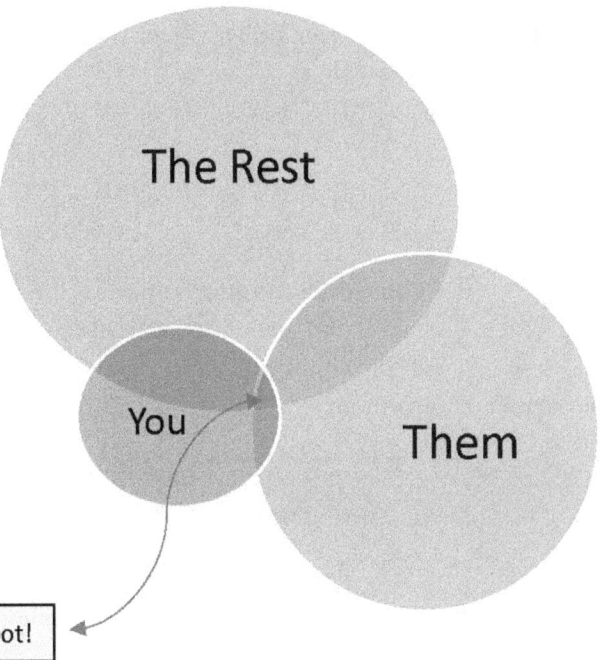

The Rest / **You** / **Them**

Your Sweet Spot!

¿Vale la pena ser potente?!

| "POWER" (and the desire for it) | ≠ (when not) | Driven By Connection | = (results in) | Failed Hierarchies and erosion of belief in 'Just Authority' and 'Mutual Respect' |

The idea of "Authority Over (+++) Other Types of Predictable Safety" leads us to the question:

"Is your safety connected to POWER? Or is it due to the authority gained by respectful connection?"

Q: Where do connection and intimacy come from?

- Mutual Affection
- Shared Experience
- Ethical Treatment
- Honesty
- Self-awareness
- Desire
- Curiosity
- Proximity (of place, time)
- Similarity of Perspective
- Healthy Boundaries
- ACCEPTANCE
- RESPECT

⚠️ **TOLERANCE** comes when we understand when we are treating others with respect and acceptance.

Emmett Till's story demonstrates how our ideas of others contribute to our treatment of them:

⬇

FETISHIZATION:

Our **desire/experience** for or of another can become entwined with our ideas of who they are, as opposed to who they are. Usually this creates a reservoir of **HIDDEN EMOTIONAL RESPONSES**.

CONTROL:

A demand for compliance without offering respect is often the product of our fetishized experience of another: their personhood, their actions and motivations become fictions, their lives subject to re-interpretation.

⚠️

Don't underestimate privacy as a solution to our over-attentiveness to the lives of others.

-- Attention that is not reciprocated can become a source of obsessive interest and fetishization --

Social Media makes good 'relationship hygiene' – self-awareness combined with an ability to avoid anti-social behavior – essential, b/c social media represents a very incomplete, inorganic type of awareness of another person.

SOCIAL MEDIA MEDIA LIST
(so meta!)

- Robocop (original w\ Peter Weller)
- Witching and Bitching
- 1984
- Taxi Driver
- The Spanish Prisoner
- Man in the Iron Mask
- Heathers
- The Lives of Others
- Neon Demon
- It Chooses You

As the use of artificial intelligence in our daily lives grows...

→

...we are increasingly reliant on mathematical or quantitative analyses to make sense of our world. Quantitative analyses coupled with historical awareness seems to result in better assessments of the people in our:

- professional life
- romantic life
- social life

Q: What judgments would people make about you if they didn't know you? What about if they only 'know' you online? Where do their perceptions of you come from?

Q: Is our idea of "normal" a product of familiarity?

¿ulpsp?!... page 2

why...

Life on Earth   >   BOOTBot Army Life

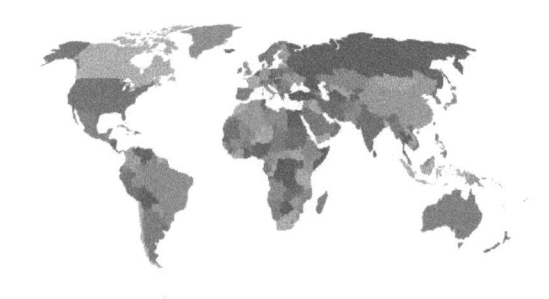

SPONTANEITY

(–) To go FWD, I have to CTRL-V or document for review?

(+) Fuck yeah, let's go!

RENEWABLE ENERGY

(+) Feeling pretty hungry. Want to grab a bite?

(–) Non-replaceable battery! EXP DATE of 1-4 years?!

PAY THE COST TO BE THE BOSS

(+) Conversation is free, data/talk/text costs $$

(–) You get to choose:
- Apple :: Apple, or
- Apple :: Banana

(–) Without in-flight devices, we are left with...

PORTABILITY

(+) Call Enterprise, they'll beam you up.

(–) Airport outlets are sometimes rarer than male squirrels!

Life on Earth is **A-OK** because

♥ ♥ people ♥ ♥

... can ignore legacy programs with obsolete operating systems without deprecating them!

Ha! LOLZ!

- True DAT

> "Where did I put that MS-DOS boot disk??"

MOVEMENT

⚠ INSTRUCTION: WHEN REACH LOWEST COMMON DENOMINATOR, ≠ PASS GO, DO NOT COLLECT 200

"When did you succumb?"

During the

Beethoven 9th
Final Movement

① LAW / ILLEGAL » ② LAW/ETHICS / ILLEGAL / UNETHICAL

⚠ (SEE INSTRUCTIONS)

These are some of the movements that make up our current moment: *Our Moment*

- Romanticism
- Transcendentalism
- ✓ Utilitarianism
- Impressionism
- Realism
- Minimalism
- Militarism
- ✓ Populism
- Platonism
- Collectivism
- Colonialism
- Feminism
- Environmentalism
- ✓ Post-modernism
- Extremism
- Abstract Expressionism
- High Modernism
- Totalitarianism
- Pacifism

NUANCE IS NOT A NEW PHENOMENON

The more we GROUP, the less of it exists

Q: "How do you prefer to engage? In groups, or more intimately?"

A: Arts/Culture, Music, Community Groups, Online, Starfleet, Affinity Groups, Political Organization, Outdoors, Traveling, Acts of Service, Over Food & Nourishment

These movements go in different 'directions' but exist simultaneously. Do you??

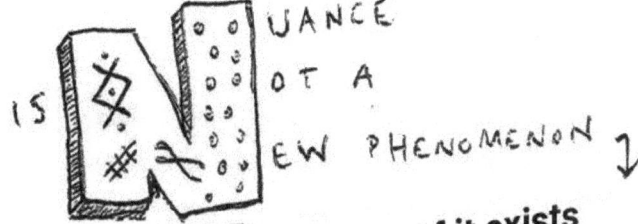

who...

Authenticity Continuum: Convince or Coerce?

Who, What and How to Want (How We Compel and Convince):

PRINCIPAL APPETITES: **Hunger – Thirst – Desire**

Core Concern: Healthy or unhealthy?

DECISIONMAKING: **Discernment – Nuance – Taste**

Core Concern: Is there a broad range of distinctions being made?

PERSONALITY AND IDENTITY: **Stability – Authenticity – Charisma**

Core Concern: Are these coherent, mutable or dynamic in social contexts?

In our social relationships, we are often part of groups, organizations, communities or systems that give our actions meaning.

- The degree of conflict we encounter in social relationships can affect our willingness to engage openly
- Social relationships depend on shared goals: our activity can be goal/mission-based, task or project-oriented, and more or less formally structured (casual).
- The dynamism of our social relationships often depends on how rules for that group are made and enforced.

> **Where You Belong:**
>
> - When I'm around people that make me feel cared for, I start to appreciate all the small actions that help me feel included.
> - Think about how you feel in the different social relationships you encounter every day: Why do you feel included?
> - Are your relationships governed by affinity, physical location or membership rules?

Dis New Who?

more on... Authenticity, Inauthenticity and Trustworthiness

Let's discuss the dangers of:

❶ Narcissists (Unconscious Victimizers)

For some, difficulty maintaining friendships and relationships is due to:

- a tendency to burn bridges, and/or
- an inability to mend fences/bridges.

People who cannot sustain relationships find it difficult to value relationships, leading to a lack of trustworthiness.

Trustworthiness is one type of authenticity that matters to tolerant people, in particular. Trustworthiness supports:

- mutual understanding and value of shared experience;
- faith that a person is not misrepresenting themselves in ways that would prejudicially affect you in social situations, in particular;
- our ability to navigate and manage expectations with others.

In addition:

- faith that a person sees you as a whole person – instead of as an idea or label – improves with trust, as does your ability to tell if others value the relationship for shared reasons;
- direct and open communication improves with trust;
- we can be more spontaneous, and experience others' spontaneity (relatively) free from anxiety, with high levels of trust;
- with trust, tolerance can be the foundation for our interactions, regardless of context – giving us more space to 'be ourselves'.

❷ Lack of Earnestness

"For many, earnestness is a way to avoid situations, especially emotionally powerful ones, that tend to have pre-determined outcomes. Earnestness is at the heart of our ability to change, because it allows others to maintain trust."

continue to page 2 ➡

Dis New Phone

The Earnestness and Authenticity Continuum:

STEREOTYPICALITY ◄————————► **EARNESTNESS**

- Inability to use language that supports authentic self-expression
- Decreased ability to interpret another's behavior and motivations ('friend or foe?')
- Inability to be experienced as a whole person (in both directions)
- Difficulty projecting the appearance of maturity

- More relationships based on voluntary association and shared goals
- Better/clearer hindsight, leading to development and growth
- Higher levels of intimacy (lasting)
- More space to be yourself without fear of judgment
- More balance between thoughts and emotions

⚠️ RACE RELATIONS in particular are damaged by stereotypicality, in part because race-based conventions for behavior are so emotionally unhealthy.

... Narcissism (Day 125)

...An Uncanny ¢urrency Story

What I Wish My Grandfather Had Told My Dad, His Stepson

"Won ore too Manny WAZE 2 dew three (3) things!"

30-Second Novel

A Play (in One Act) on Words

"Identity and Rules, the Interplay"

Paige 1: "Identify yourself rules."

> --- **Family Fuel'd** ---
>
> **FEIGNED STATES OF OFFENSE**
> (Top Wrong Answers on the Board)
>
> ① Undesirable Stance
>
> ② Undesirable Outcome
>
> ③ Large Vocabulary
>
> ④ "In the Lost City of Awareness"

🖤 🖤 **The Lost City of Awareness, part 8702.4** 🖤 🖤

In the land where I was born... some people took a road trip and forgot to leave their breadcrumbs. Instead of making them save chicken bones, we posed some identifying questions!

- Sometimes we block certain truths out of our awareness. If one of those truths is... My Favorite Smoothie Recipe or The Name of My Best Friends' Favorite Song, is this a problem? When would we forget the friend, if we let this happen?
- What do you wish your grandparents had told your dad? Or your aunt, mother, brother or sister?

>>> A Recipe for Miss D. Aster <<<

> "A stake through the heart of feigned ignorance!"

Humans can hear variances in sound between 18Hz and 18-19 kHz, and some of those sounds sound like the album "Ambient 4: On Land" by Brian Eno.

See if you can finish this sentence!

"If I were a musician, my favorite book/song/meal would be..."

Lenses
...(Hindsight being 20/10)

Ways to:

Identify the Territories Beyond the Personal (aka Shared Spaces):

- Interpersonal
- Group
- Organizational
- Systems
  - Process
  - Dynamics and Outcomes
- Transformations

Assess a Frame – Is It:

- Rhetorical/Linguistic
- Complexity-based
- Abstraction-based
- Emotional Range-based
- Process- vs. Outcomes-based
- Logical Style-based
- Ego/Agency-based
- Magnitude of Effect/Size Scale-based
- Ingroup/Outgroup-based
- Cooperative/Uncooperative-based
- Technical/Mystical
- Qualitative/Quantitative
- Hierarchy-based

Q: Does everything that is communicated become abstract or subject to abstraction through language? What are the implications?

Q: How much do claims of agency matter, when we discuss 1) events or 2) ideas?

Q: Do we all have 'sensory hierarchies' – principal ways we experience the world?

How Would You Describe Your Context?

Many Lenses and Perspectives Are Contextual:

- Controlled contexts
- Uncontrolled/unrestricted contexts
- Experimental/playful contexts
- Evaluation or assessment contexts

Assessments of Contexts Can Be:

- **Philosophical** (with considerations for beneficiaries, equity, morality/ethicality, desirability)
- **Aesthetic** (with considerations for beauty (geometric), harmony, melody, cacophony, cultural assessments of beauty that create desirability)
- **Practical** (with consideration of profitability, usefulness, legality, inevitability, desirability, harmoniousness, sustainability)

Section 3
Worksheets

This worksheet is based on the principles in the #blowpop curriculum, as a complement to the POGMAHON unit.

Complete by _____

What (Eye) See:

Your Top ⑤ Answers on the Board:

PRIORITIES

- ☐ Job
- ☐ Family
- ☐ Personal Growth & Development
- ☐ Friends
- ☐ Financial Security
- ☐ Lifestyle

> - **Priorities** – What's important?
> - **Objectives** – What do you want to accomplish?
> - **Groupthink, Insight or Anticipation** – Are you considering your past, present or future?
> - **Meaning** – What does this mean and why? Am I reacting to the moment?
> - **Analysis** – Really? Why do I think this? Would I believe it if I were being honest about my assessment?
> - **Honesty** – I'm being honest about the facts and whom I represent.
> - **Open to Change** – Are there opportunities for growth?
> - **Next Steps**

OBJECTIVES (in song)

- ☐ "Bear Necessities!"
- ☐ Hart to Hart
- ☐ Automatic for the People
- ☐ "Reel Love"
- ☐ Other _____
- ☐ Other _____

WHAT (EYE) SEE

When I look around, I see: Indicate whether or not it is "same" or "different", and how much what you see pleases you on a scale of 1-7.

_____ RATING ____

_____ RATING ____

_____ RATING ____

_____ RATING ____

WHAT I BRING TO THE TABLE (Linens provided at no charge!)

_____   _____

_____   _____

BONUS: Your Professional Hazards are:

_____   _____

_____   _____

Q: If the person who cared about you the most knew what you wanted most for yourself, would they feel you were making good choices?

Q: Do your dream, waking and fantasy (unrealistic or realistic) lives align in any meaningful way?

Q: Where in your life do you find the most meaning? What assumptions does your idea of meaning rest on?

YOUR PREFERRED MODE

"A" might be where you find community but "B" might be what keeps you engaged:

"A" – Conscientious Selection based on:

- ☐ Mental Habits
- ☐ Pattern Recognition (Behavior)
- ☐ Growth Mindset
- ☐ Social Capital
- ☐ Currency of Social Capital

"B" – In my community, I fill these roles: (To refine your answers, try identifying "Wrong Answers Only" and "When I Care Enough to Care")

_____   _____

_____   _____

_____   _____

We often focus on other people's roles when we want to maintain boundaries that keep relationships transactional.

"Relationships are not paid speaking engagements or volunteer/community service opportunities!"

IS IT BIG AND BLUE?

❶ What do YOU plan to do with this mess? How important is this plan to you?

_____ IMPORTANCE ____

_____ IMPORTANCE ____

_____ IMPORTANCE ____

_____ IMPORTANCE ____

_____ IMPORTANCE ____

❷ FINAL QUESTION: TRU or FAULSE?

"Personhood for everyone" should be everyone's goal:

☐ T
☐ F

Canary Knows! Inner Motivations for Assumption's Most Devout

(A) Where does Understanding Come from?
reflection
experience
observation
education
sensation integration
connection

(B) Self-awareness ← too

(E) Subjectivity

(C) Scientific Self-awareness
↑
Objectivity

Signs symbols
sense (time, space)
simultaneity
sensation
+ shared simultaneity

(H) Awareness of another's subjectivity as something ≠ object

↳ TRUE PRESENCE

Λ + Ω

(D) Where does DIVERSITY of perspective come from?

"The music we share can be experienced as harmony, even when the orchestra is AT REST."

≈ //// MOST LIKELY SOURCES //// ≈

• EXP REVERSE-ENGINEERED FROM OBSERVATION w/ ___novelty___
                                      x percent

• 'OBSERVATION EXPLAINED USING DIVERSITY OF PERSPECTIVE'.
Which reveals the stories we have to SHARE

❝❝ Their words...

combine with a perception grounded in historical human needs for connection,

THE AUTHOR WISHES YOU TO KNOW

David J. Shepard melds fiction, non-fiction, journalism, poetry and content marketing techniques to depict the awareness of a thoroughly modern mind. Genre-agnosticism and hybrid forms reveal a literary world where texts are "content." In his work, popular culture is a point of departure for discussions of race, identity and difference.

-Artist Biography-

A native son of Boston (Mass.), David resides reluctantly in a present that is tense. He has traveled to more than 40 other cities in the U.S. and Europe. Born a poor Black child, David has followed his curiosity to earnest engagement with people from six continents who value connection, trust, respect and openness.

Also from Internet Ouroboros/Ouroboros Press

#Blessed be THE HELLBOUND
by Uppity Atom and Uncanny Currency

All Day Sucker
by David J. Shepard

SUPPORT
BLACK OWNED
BUSINESSES